T0290392

Gambiered Canton Gauze:
Ethereal Silk Fabric from South China

Elegant Guangdong Series Editorial Board

Paths International Ltd

南方日报出版社
NANFANG DAILY PRESS

CONTENTS

Union of Heaven and Man
The Dyeing and Finishing Process

A Reborn Artifact
Development Dilemma and Prospect

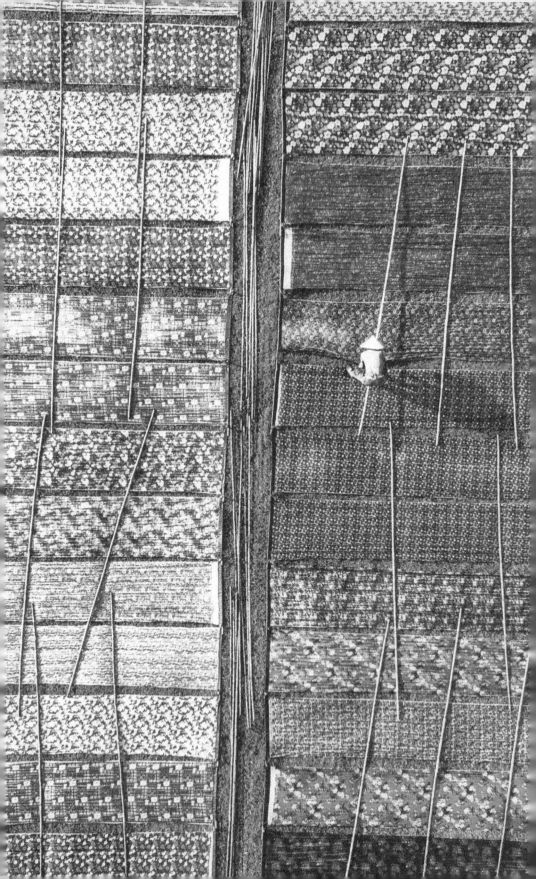

Foreword

"When lychee ripens, cicada chirps, the gambiered Canton gauze rustles; sugarcanes roll, plantain leaves ruffle, in gambiered gauze I luxuriates." Gambiered Canton gauze is an ancient species of dyed gauze produced in the Pearl River Delta area. The gauze is a kind of permeable, refreshing and light fabric, which brings about cooling effect to the wearer. As the gauze gives off the "rustling" sound in walking, it was originally named "rustling gauze".

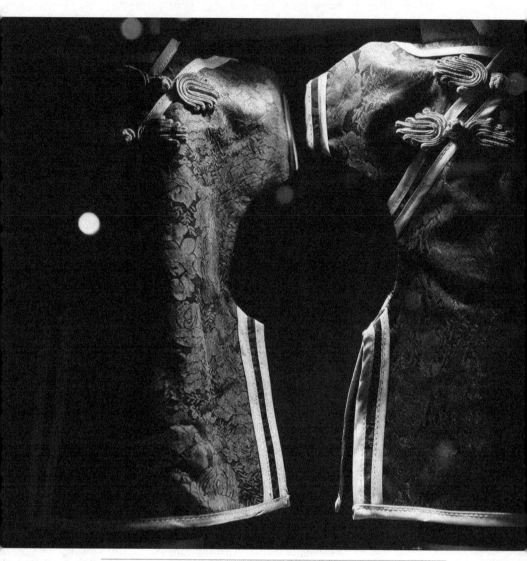

A cultural enterprise in Shenzhen sells clothing made from gambiered Canton gauze at home and abroad

Complicated production process and special silk texture brings the repute of "soft gold" to gambiered Canton gauze. History has seen the exorbitant price of 12 taels of silver trading for a bolt of gauze. It is the worthy peak of "perfection" in the realm of silk. The gauze differs from other silks in that its mellowness is like fine wine over time, the more you wear the more charming it turns. Contact with skin will induce a chemical reaction in the fabric of the gauze; it will gradually show its isabellinus grounding. The longer you wear, the finer the grain on the surface will develop, the more oily and glossy black it will show, as though it has come alive.

The gauze has drawn many loyal fans, the Soong Sisters were the best known among them. The Soong Ching Ling Memorial Hall in Shanghai displayed Soong Ching Ling's favorite black cheongsam which is made of gambiered Canton gauze. This cheongsam had been with her on many public occasions. When she gained weight as she aged, Soong Ching Ling had the cheongsam let out for continuing wear. Her deep love for the cloth could be seen therefrom. In the 1920s, many socialites including Eileen Chang, Lu Xiaoman, Wang Yingxia were all fans of the gauze. Eileen Chang not only put the gauze on the her novel characters, but also chose pictures of gambiered Canton gauze as accompanying illustrations of her English book *Chinese Life and Fashions*. Due to rarity of the fabric, it is said that a mother would hand sew a set of gauze clothes as dowry for her daughter at her marriage. When the daughter gets old, she would then bequeath the gauze as a family heirloom to her offspring.

Gauze drying

The appearance of gambiered Canton gauze marked an important milestone in the history of China's two-millennia long silk product development, which brought about the glory attained in the histories of silk industry and silk trade of Guangdong province. In 2008, the gambiered Canton gauze was placed into the catalog of national intangible cultural heritage for its unique dyeing and finishing technology. At a time where people are paying growing attention to ideas of environment protection and preservation of traditional technology, the characteristics of naturalness from the source of materials to production has won back customers' attention and favor.

Birth and Evolution

Origin of
Gambiered Canton Gauze

Source
Mulberry-Fish Ecosystem Laying Foundation for
the Birth of the Gauze

First Encounter
Yam Juice Dyed Gauze Blackening
When Exposed to Mud

Source

Mulberry-Fish Ecosystem Laying Foundation for the Birth of the Gauze

The Encyclopedia of China—Volume of Textile defines the gambiered Canton gauze as glossy and sleek jet-black silk fabric (dye yam gauze) with open-work florets, "the fabric is made with procedures including scouring, degumming, applying extracted dye yam solution, applying dark river mud and rinsing". In 2008, *Application Materials of Gambiered Canton Gauze for Listing in the 2nd Batch of National Intangible Cultural Heritage Catalog* holds that gambiered Canton gauze is a plain fabric silk product (silk) and a silk gauze fabric (gauze) after dyeing and finishing processes. There are differences in the scope of the two concepts; however, they have two points in common: first, they are made of silk; second, they are products processed with dyeing and finishing techniques.

Gauze drying

Mulberry planting, silkworm breeding, silk reeling and silk weaving are traditional industries with a long history of over two thousand years in the Pearl River Delta. The special environment of interlacing rivers in the Pearl River Delta area gives rise to a unique agricultural ecological chain, the "mulberry-fish ecosystem". It is a work of wisdom created by the local people. They grow mulberries and raise silkworms on fish pond banks. The silkworm's feces and their chrysalis can feed fish, while pond mud turns further into manure to fertilize the mulberry, hence a repeatable cycle is formed. Due to the tremendous profit obtained from raising silkworm and weaving silk, during the period from the Ming Dynasty to the Qing Dynasty, there occurred three rushes of building fish ponds by destroying crop land and planting mulberry by scraping rice paddies in Pearl River Delta. These rushes brought about well-developed mulberry and silkworm production bases, which in turn ushered in the progress of industries such as silk reeling and silk weaving.

By the Ming Dynasty, silk products from Guangdong had already made their name across the nation. According to *Annals of Guangzhou Prefecture* in the reign of emperor Qianlong, "Canton silk is superior to that of Jinling (Nanjing nowadays), Suzhou and Hangzhou." However, raw silk for the weaving industry were mainly shipped in from the Suzhou-Hangzhou area, as silk from that place was of better quality, and silk fabric weaved with such silk was superior in color and luster to that weaved with locally purchased silk. Since the Opium War of 1840, the Qing government opened five additional trading ports including

Gambiered Canton gauze neatly drying in the sun

Shanghai, which practically shattered Guangzhou's status as the "sole trading port". Export of silk produced in the Suzhou-Hangzhou area was no longer conducted via Guangzhou, instead Shanghai in close vicinity was chosen as the export port for such silk. After the breakout of the Taiping Heavenly Kingdom Movement, trade routes between the various places were cut off, however, international demand for silk remained strong. Guangdong merchants had to count on local silk producers for the production of silk fabric, which facilitated the rapid growth of mulberry and silk industries.

First Encounter

Yam Juice Dyed Gauze Blackening When Exposed to Mud

As a superior plant dyeing material for bronzing, the commonly available dye yam in the mountainous areas of Lingnan (south of the Five Ridges) had been put to use by the local people. In his works *Mengxi Bitan (Dream Pool Essays)*, Shen Kuo of the North Song Dynasty recorded the local practice of people living there dyeing leather for shoes with dye yam. Practices of dyeing fishnet, rope, cloth with dye yam can be found in literature thereafter. However, the earliest definite record of employing dye yam as a silk fabric dye material appeared in *The County Annals of Panyu* in the third year of the Xuantong period (1911), "the people of Shiqiao town mostly grow dye yams as a means of livelihood, which is used as a

Gambiered Canton gauze is dyed
with dye yams and then dried

dye material in the making of dye yam gauze", and "the dye yam gauze produced therefrom made its name known far and wide". The so-called dye yam gauze is the end silk product resulting from applying extracted dye yam solution. The fact indicates that there had already been gambiered Canton gauze in the broad sense in the Qing Dynasty.

The silk fabric appears bronzing after dyeing process with dye yam. Apply river mud and let the iron element undergo a delicate reaction with the dye yam solution, only after this process can a resin-like purely natural black membrane be formed on the side whereon river mud is applied. This is the critical step in the entire dyeing and finishing process—mud application. Some researchers hold that, the mud application process is inspired by the fact that fishermen discovered that fishnet turns black when it is taken from water and aired.

Fishermen in the Pearl River Delta are fond of dyeing fishnet with dye yam to make it more resilient, moisture-resistant and corrosion-resistant. Qu Dajun recorded in *New Remarks on Guangdong* the following: "the dye yam solution is red, it turns black when it comes in contact with water. The fish pertains to the virtue of fire, hence it favors water; the water is of black color, hence it accords with the nature of the fish." Researchers analyzed the phenomenon according to this entry and proposed that, the fact fishnet turns black when coming into contact with water is that fishnet comes into contact with mud on riverbed and mud is rinsed off when the fishnet is pulled out of water. The process is like applying and rinsing mud. Having finished a fishing trip, the fishermen air dried their fishnets in the sun, iron in the mud reacted with the dye yam juice in the fishnet, the fishnet finally turned black. Through observation and analysis of the color change of the fishnet in the process, people invented the mud application technique and applied the dyeing and finishing technique to production of gambiered Canton gauze, which turns the front side of the fabric into glossy and lustrous black.

Gauze dyeing

Union of Heaven and Man

The Dyeing and Finishing Process

Material
Naturally Endowed and Locally Sourced

Procedures
Craftsmanship and Ingenuity

Material

Naturally Endowed and Locally Sourced

The dyeing and finishing process of gambiered Canton gauze follows ancient technological requirements handed down for hundreds of years. The three key factors include dye yam juice, river mud and sunlight, none of which is not naturally obtainable. The silk greige, of which gauze is made, is woven with silk produced by silkworm. It is justifiable to say that the gambiered Canton gauze is an artistic treasure endowed by nature to the people living south of the Five Ridges .

Gambiered Canton gauze originates from Shunde

The silk greige could be classified into two categories: "the white silk greige" and "the white gauze greige", according to the texture and grain of silk greige. "The white silk greige" refers to plain weave texture silk products, or raw silk, it is a kind of fine and even texture; "guaze", folk name for which is "the white gauze greige", refers to skein silk products woven with jacquard which had been innovated by craftsmen from Nanhai County in the early years of the Republic of China, featuring fretwork of jacquard weave. There are myriad pores on the fabric, which makes it all the more fit for wear in the humid and sultry weather of Guangdong area.

Shunde gambiered Canton gauze Eco-Agricultural Park

Dye yam is the tuber of a vine plant that grows in the remote mountains of subtropical regions, and is most commonly seen in Guangdong and Guangxi. Its tuber skin is of dark brown color and bumpy appearance. If you cut it open, you will find that the inside is dark red or reddish yellow. The dye yam is widely used in traditional Chinese medicine. It can be used to stop bleeding, relieve pain and sterilize. Its tuber juice is rich in tannin, which is the basic dyeing material for gambiered Canton gauze.

For a long time, the gambiered Canton gauze could only be produced in Shunde, Nanhai and other places in the Pearl River Delta area, because there is another indispensable material for making the gambiered Canton gauze, which is not the ordinary river mud, but unpolluted river mud with iron element presence. This kind of mud is only available in rivers of the Pearl River Delta area. The river mud in these areas has not been polluted and is very fine and smooth. Therefore, although Japan and other countries have tried to produce gambiered Canton gauze in their own countries, they have all ended up in failure due to the fact that the river mud, the key material for forming the black and shiny coating on the gauze, cannot be replicated.

Making gambiered Canton gauze is a craft that depends on the climate. The silk impregnated with dye yam juice must be repeatedly exposed to the sun to allow the tannin in the dye yam juice to fully penetrate the white gauze greige and deposit a coating on the surface of the cloth. If it rains while drying, the rain will produce a piece of cloth unevenly colored. Only April to October are the time when the weather of Guangdong is fit for drying the gauze with long and adequate sunlight. In July and August, the sunshine is too strong and the temperature is too high; in such weather, the gauze dried tends to be rigid and brittle, which is not the ideal time to commence production. In November, the dry northern monsoon blows southward, so it is also not suitable for drying the gauze. Therefore, the time fit for drying the gauze is no more than four months in a year.

The sun shines on gambiered Canton gauze

Procedures

Craftsmanship and Ingenuity

The dyeing and finishing technique of the gambiered Canton gauze is also called "gauze drying". It consists of 14 main processes, including preparation of silk greige, soaking with dye yam juice, drying, sealing dye yam solution, boiling and extracting, applying river mud, rinsing, stretching fabric, absorbing fog moisture, rolling silk, packing and warehousing. The entire process is very complicated and cumbersome, relying entirely on manual work. It generally takes about 15 days to complete the whole process. Regardless of the concentration of dye yam juice, or the number of times of drying and sealing, each process can only be adjusted by the skilled craftsmen with reference to experience. The craftsman makes timely adjustments according to the specific situation, "varying adjustments on different weathers, different places, different workshops, different handling personnel", which makes every bolt of gambiered Canton gauze unique in its own way.

There are key steps in the dyeing and finishing process of gambiered Canton gauze as follows:

The first step is preparing dye yam juice. Grind the dye yam, immerse it in a trough to extract yam juice, filter out the yam dregs, and pour the solution in a large wooden barrel for later use. Silks of different qualities and different weaving techniques have different requirements for the concentration of yam solution. The quality of prepared yam solution is the key to determining the quality of gambiered Canton gauze. There is no established standard for the concentration of the dye yam solution. The craftsmen in charge of preparation adjust the concentration according to the quantity of fabric to be dyed and finished and the speed of dyeing and finishing everyday as they see fit. The concentration for a specific use relies exclusively on the experience of the craftsmen accumulated over the years, and there is no guidebook to refer to.

Finished gambiered Canton gauze

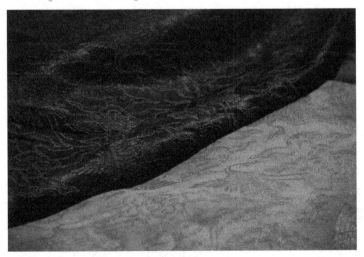

Gauze drying

The second step is soaking and drying. A bolt of silk is cut into 20-meter pieces (fit for handling by one person), and placed in a sink filled with yam solution. The craftsmen begin to stir continuously the silk with their hands to make the silk fully soaked and absorb the yam solution evenly. The silk is then taken out of the tank and aired naturally; after that the silk is unfolded and straightened out on the lawn, exposed to the sun until dry. After the silk is dried, in order to make the dye more evenly, the workers will spray yam solution on the silk from a bucket. The sprayed yam solution will then be swept with a cattail broom to spread it evenly on the silk fabric. The process of drying, soaking and redrying will be repeated many times.

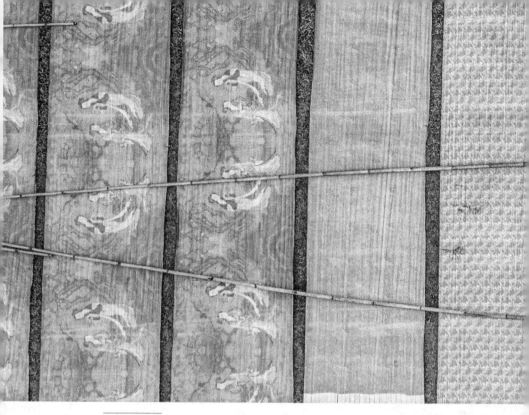

Gauze drying

The function of drying silk on the grass is that the silk can absorb a certain amount of moisture from the grass when exposed to high temperature, while the silk can be kept clean when it is kept away from soil and sand by the grass beneath. Furthermore, the substantial temperature difference between the front side and the back side of silk can enhance the "two-tone colour" contrastive effect of gambiered Canton gauze. Therefore, grass for such purpose must be soft, which would not scratch the silk fabric, while it can support a certain weight. Therefore, the grass cultivated for drying gambiered Canton gauze is generally trimmed to 1–2 centimeters high. The local grass species with the folk name of "ground-crawling mouse" is fit for this purpose.

The third step is applying river mud. This process is the key to silk drying process. Extract river mud unique to the rivers of the Pearl River Delta area, stir it into a evenly mixed paste, and apply the paste evenly on the front side of the silk with a specially made mop. The silk covered with river mud is then lifted in tightly stretched state to the grass by two workers. The silk then sits still for half an hour. This process can ensure that the high-valent iron ions in the river mud and the tannin in the yam solution induce sufficient chemical reaction to produce black precipitates that condense on the front side of the fabric. In eras prior to the creation of greenhouses which can provide shade and shelter, in order to allow sufficient time for the chemical reaction to take place between river mud and the silk, the "mud application" process had to be completed before sunrise.

After the mud application process, the silk must be moved to the river immediately to wash off the remaining river mud on the fabric, and then it will be spread flat on the grass again. At this time, the sun has just risen and the early morning sun can dry the silk. By this time, the front side of the silk covered with river mud displays a black and oily appearance, adding a pottery-like luster, while the back side still remains reddish brown because it has not been exposed to the river mud.

The fourth step is to spread out the silk to absorb fog moisture. After the sun goes down in the evening, dew condenses and forms on the grass. At this time, the rigid silk fabric after mud application and drying is spread again on the grass to absorb moisture from the grass. The silk gradually softens. This process is called "spreading out for fog moisture absorption".

Fog moisture absorption is the last process; however, the gambiered Canton gauze being processed thus far is still not yet the final product. After steps of rolling, measuring, packing and committing to warehouse, it will then sit in the warehouse for 3–6 months before being moved for the next step process.

Finished gambiered Canton gauze

A Reborn Artifact

*Development Dilemma
and Prospect*

Slump
Dwindling Enthusiasm in the Transmission
of Tradition

Breakthrough
Improvement Propped by the Fashion Industry

Slump

Dwindling Enthusiasm in the Transmission of Tradition

The entirely hand-made craftsmanship, combined with time, location and people, have made gambiered Canton gauze unreplicable, which has also made it the bottleneck in gambiered Canton gauze's inheritance. Mr. Liang Zhu, the inheritor of the craft, explained that the reliance of skills in making gambiered Canton gauze on the elements requires the inheritor to be very careful and demands a high degree of attention, a little misstep would jeopardize the entire process.

A fashion show of gambiered Canton gauze

Long time exposure to the sun in the production of gambiered Canton gauze entails intensive hard labor. Take the most primitive and most ancient practice of "drying gauze" for instance, in order to achieve the optimal two-tone colour contrast effect between the front side and the back side, workers had to work from 3 a.m. to 4 p.m. during the period from the beginning of April to the end of October each year—the hottest season in places south of the Five Ridges and yet the best time for drying gauze. Workers had to endure fatigue and scorching weather, and had to repeat the airing and drying process. In order to obtain even dyeing effect of the silk, workers had to work with almost no break throughout the day, carrying out spreading,

35

Exquisite gambiered Canton gauze decoration

After the process is improved, the gambiered Canton gauze with both texture, beauty and fashion sense

straightening, spraying water, and contracting processes. Therefore, there are very few people who have really mastered the know-how in making gambiered Canton gauze in modern times, and those who have mastered tend to be old, while young people are unwilling to learn the trade. Whether future generations can inherit and continue the legend of the gambiered Canton gauze is really a grave issue that the industry currently faces.

Another dilemma is the problem of market demand. The 1930s was the heyday of gambiered Canton gauze production. The production scale was very large, with up to ten thousand workers employed. However, with the rise of market substitutes, such as chemical fibers and textiles, the output of gambiered Canton gauze dwindled year by year. By the 1980s, many gambiered Canton gauze factories closed down or switched business. At present, there are only three professional producers of gambiered Canton gauze in the country, and they are mainly aimed at foreign markets.

Breakthrough

Improvement Propped by the Fashion Industry

Mr. Liang Zhu, who is over 80 years old, worked as an apprentice in gambiered Canton gauze factory at the age of 14, and has witnessed the ups and downs of the development of gambiered Canton gauze. In the 1990s, in order to preserve the gambiered Canton gauze craft, he bought the closed gambiered Canton gauze factory. With accumulated experience, he innovated the gauze drying process on the basis of traditional crafts, developed the process of "three washings, nine cookings and eighteen dryings". His gambiered Canton gauze gradually won market's recognition and many overseas orders.

Gambiered Canton gauze's Clothing Store

With the forceful support from Lunjiao government agency of Shunde municipality, in 2007 the "gambiered Canton gauze drying process", that is, the "gambiered Canton gauze dyeing and finishing technique" was successfully declared a provincial intangible cultural heritage, and in 2008 it was elevated and placed on the catalog of the second batch of national intangible cultural heritage. Furthermore, there are young people willing to learn the dyeing and finishing process of gambiered Canton gauze and apprentice with Mr. Liang Zhu to take on the mantle.

Gambiered Canton gauze's works exhibited at the 2016 Fashion Management EMBA Academic Exchange Conference

Shunde designer Qu Tingnan, one of China's top ten fashion designers, curator of the Lingnan Costume Museum and inheritor of Guangzhou embroidery, who grew up next to a drying factory, developed a deep affection for gambiered Canton gauze. He has been committed to the development and inheritance of the gambiered Canton gauze craft. He participated in the clothing design competition organized by the United Nations with design work based on gambiered Canton gauze, and won the "World Folk Culture Award". His effort won the approval from international experts and helped the world rediscover the gambiered Canton gauze.

Gambiered Canton gauze runway show

Furthermore, Qu Tingnan also asked experts to develop a variety of colors of gambiered Canton gauze, and successfully developed a red cuit silk. In 2018, in the China International Fashion Week, Qu Tingnan's "Scent, Auspice, Sound and Direction" theme fashion show featured high-end fashion clothes made of colorful gambiered Canton gauze fabric, which brought Chinese intangible cultural art—gambiered Canton gauze—back on the world stage again.

Gambiered Canton gauze, the beautiful fabric inherited and developed by several generations or even more than a dozen generations, will serve as a time-honored business card of foreign exchanges. In the time where values such as tradition, return to nature and environment protection are cherished, it has, with its characteristics of naturalness, blazed a path of design which perfectly blends the locality of culture and the cosmopolitan nature of fashion, and gained increasing popularity among Chinese and people around the world.

The Exquisite 8, dress made of gambiered Canton gauze collected in China National Silk Museum

This book is the result of a co-publication agreement between Nanfang Daily Press (CHINA) and Paths International Ltd. (UK)

Title: Gambiered Canton Gauze: Ethereal Silk Fabric from South China
Author: Elegant Guangdong Series Editorial Board
Hardback ISBN: 978-1-84464-727-9
Paperback ISBN: 978-1-84464-728-6
Ebook ISBN: 978-1-84464-729-3
Copyright © 2022 by Paths International Ltd., UK and by Nanfang Daily Press, China

Paths International Ltd
www.pathsinternational.com

Published in United Kingdom

CPSIA information can be obtained
at www.ICGtesting.com
Printed in the USA
LVHW081256080223
738262LV00001B/3